Softball Basics: All About Softball

ISBN-13: 978-1480000117
ISBN-10: 1480000116

Copyright Notice

SOFTBALL BASICS: ALL ABOUT SOFTBALL

Lucy Boscombe

I dedicate this to the lucky people who've been touched by the fun, excitement and buzz of softball...

Contents

Softball:
A Brief History

Softball is undoubtedly one of the world's most popular sports.

In the United States alone, there are about 25 to 40 million people who play the game, which has been part of the Olympic Games since 1996.

Before it gained worldwide popularity, though, softball was played only by a few young men back in 1887.

They were waiting for the results of a football match between Harvard and Yale when one of these young men threw a boxing glove at his friend, who then hit the glove with a pole.

George Hancock then tied the glove up to resemble a ball and grabbed a broomstick handle before shouting, "Let's play ball!"

The score in that first softball game was an amazing 41-40 and Hancock is now known as the father of softball.

In the following years, Hancock worked on refining the game. The glove was replaced with a real ball and the broomstick handle with a rubber-tipped bat.

He also wrote down a set of rules for the new game.

The game was then named indoor baseball because, you've guessed it right, it was originally played indoors.

And then, in 1895, fire department officer Lewis Rober, Sr. of Minneapolis designed a similar game in an effort to provide his men with a way of staying active even when they weren't on duty.

He called his game 'kitten' to honour the very first team that played it.

It was only in 1926 when the game was finally given the name 'softball' by Walter Hakanson of the YMCA at a National Recreation Congress meeting.

It took several years for other people to pick up the new name, though.

Softball only became popularly called by its present name in the United States in 1930.

And owing to the fact that the game was still relatively new at the time, the different leagues in different areas played by different rules.

Finally, the Joint Rules Committee was established in 1934 and the game got its official and standardized rules and name.

Softball competitions all over the world then started to be governed by the International Softball Federation in 1951.

In 1965, Australia hosted the very first world championships for women's fast pitch. A year after that, the men's championships were also held.

And world championships have been held every four years since 1970.

It is generally accepted that the year 1996 saw the peak of softball's popularity when it became part of the Olympic Games.

And even though the sport was dropped from the 2012 Summer Olympics, it still remains one of the world's most popular sports, especially in the United States.

The popularity of softball is perhaps largely due to its general appeal to people of all ages and the fact that the game is played according to different age groups.

You can definitely expect to see it maintain its popularity and mass appeal for many years to come.

The kind of development it's currently enjoying is definitely not bad for a game that began with a boxing glove and broomstick handle.

The Basics

If you want to learn how to play softball, then you should start by learning its rules.

A softball match is normally played in at least seven innings.

Each team gets a turn to bat in each inning until three of their batters are out. The decision as to which team gets to bat first is made via toss coin.

There are, however, some softball leagues that make this decision upon its discretion. The general rule in these leagues is that the home team gets to bat second.

In all softball leagues, the fielding team is considered as the defensive team whereas the batting team is the offensive team, as they're the ones who try to score runs.

The game officially begins when the umpire says, "Play Ball!"

A batter then sets up at the plate and then all fielders take their positions in fair territory, with the exception of the catcher, whose position is at the back of the plate.

The pitcher takes his position at the pitching plate, where he tries to throw the ball past the opposing team's batter straight to the waiting catcher.

Softball pitches are required to be delivered using an underarm motion.

The different types and leagues may have variations in terms of their strike zone.

All throws that pass through the strike zone is considered a strike. Any throw that's not within the strike zone and the batter doesn't swing at is called a ball.

The total number of strikes and balls is known as the count.

Whenever a ball lands in the foul area, it is called a dead ball because no plays are allowed at this time until the ball gets back in the hands of the pitcher.

Once again, the umpire declares "Play Ball" and the game resumes. Leaping is deemed illegal in softball and if the pitcher does this, the batter gets awarded a ball.

The batting order of the offensive team has to remain the same for the duration of a game. One batter at a time gets a chance to bat based on the predetermined batting order.

If a team deems substitution necessary at any time, the substitute will have to bat in the same order as the player he's substituting. In co-ed softball leagues, boys and girls are required to bat alternately.

The batter needs to stand inside the batter's box facing the pitcher. He should then hold the bat with both of his hands, with the bat's head over his shoulders and held away from the pitcher.

Whenever the batter successfully hits the ball into fair territory, he should then try to get to first base or even beyond.

At this time, the player is now known as the runner. There are still other rules that apply in a game of softball, but these are the basics you need to familiarise so you can start learning how to play the game.

In general, what makes softball so popular is the fact that its rules can easily be modified, thus making it easy for people of varying skill levels to learn.

Softball Training Equipment

If you seriously want to learn how to play softball, then you'd do well to look for some effective softball training equipment.

The good news is that there are plenty of items you can use to improve your performance in the sport.

Read on to find out what your options are in terms of softball training equipment and so you can make an informed decision as to which equipment could benefit you most.

Bats and Balls

The basic equipment needed for softball training is, of course, a set of balls and a bat. Whatever position you play, you'll have handle the ball at one point or another.

This makes it important for you to train with weighted balls that can assist you in strengthening your muscles and improving the accuracy of your throws.

Training with a heavier ball also helps increase the speed of your throw, which is indeed very helpful if you play as a pitcher and when you throw from the outfield.

When you step onto the field and handle the regulation ball, it'll feel so light that throwing would seem like child's play. You can buy a set of weighted balls for about $25.

As regards the training bat, it typically features adjustable weights hanging from the end. The weights allow you to promote muscle memory and increase the strength of your swing.

You also have the option of using a training bat for warm-up purposes.

It effectively helps your muscles loosen up before you get your turn to bat in an actual game. You can usually buy training bats for anywhere from $35 to $70.

Pitching Machines and Batting Tees

Pitching machines have certainly evolved much since they were first created several years ago.

There are now pitching machines of good quality that feed you with 30mph balls at predetermined intervals. And perhaps the best thing about these machines is that you can buy them at just about $40.

Another piece of softball training equipment you may want to consider is the batting tee, which holds the ball above the ground so you can practice your hitting skills.

The price of batting tees typically ranges from $25 to $200, depending on how sophisticated the model is.

Soft Mitts and Reaction Balls

Among the newer pieces of softball training equipment are soft mitts and reaction balls. The former are flat foam mitts used to improve coordination between your two hands.

It therefore encourages quicker transition from the task of catching to throwing the ball. This is a very good equipment to train with if you play as a fielder.

You can buy them for about $15 to $20. The reaction ball is best defined as a ball featuring bumps. The bumps make it bounce unpredictably when it hits the ground, which helps improve your reaction time as well as your hand-eye coordination.

Just like the soft mitts, this is also advisable for use by fielders.

There are other softball training equipment that can assist with improving your strength and physical condition.

Whatever pieces of equipment you choose to work with, they'll surely help you learn softball a lot quicker and in a more effective way.

Choosing the Right Bat

It's important to have the right equipment when playing softball, as this can help ensure a good performance in the game.

One of the pieces of equipment you need to choose carefully is, of course, the softball bat.

There are several different types of bat and you'll have to make sure the one you choose is specifically designed for the type of game you'll be playing as well as your own playing style.

Using the right bat allows you to play more comfortably, thus improving your overall performance during a game.

Softball bats are made in different weights and sizes to suit the different players who use them.

This means a bat that's the perfect fit for one player may not really be the perfect fit for you. This is why you need to learn how to determine if a bat is indeed right for you.

The best way for you to find the right bat is to visit a retail sporting goods store where you can actually grip the bats and get a feel for each model you consider.

Give each bat a few test swings to see if it feels right. If not, move on and try another model. Of course, you need to make sure the store has enough space for you to test the bats so you don't hit anyone or anything with them.

If you already have a bit of experience in softball and have gained an understanding of what particular bat you need to get, then you also have the option of buying your bat from an online seller.

The good thing about online stores is that they often have very good deals to offer.

Among the most important things you need to ensure if you choose to go this route is that the online store from which you get your bat has an acceptable return policy so you don't get stuck with a softball bat that really meet your specific needs in an actual game.

Now, you may wonder if it's a good idea to buy your own bat right away or if you should wait until you get more experience in the sport before doing so.

Well, the perfect time for buying your own softball bat depends entirely on your own needs.

If you're just trying out the sport and aren't really sure if it's something you can stick with for a long time, then it may not be such a good idea to buy your own bat.

However, if you're sure that you want to build a career in softball or at least that you'll be playing the game for many years to come, then it's definitely advisable to buy a bat as soon as you start training with a team.

It's a good thing if you happen to join a team just after softball season closes because this is the time when most stores put several items on sale.

You'll realise that this helps you save a considerable amount of money when you compare the prices of the same items at this time to that of their prices just before softball season starts.

If you're serious about becoming a softball player, then you should know the value of investing in a bat that's just right for you.

Choosing the Right Mitt

Among the most important pieces of softball equipment you need to choose very carefully is the softball mitt.

And the very first thing you should consider when shopping for the perfect mitt is the position you play. That's because players of differing positions also have different tasks and responsibilities.

Consequently, there are different types of mitt for the different positions in softball.

If you're still having a bit of trouble recognizing an infielder's glove from a catcher's mitt, then you'll definitely appreciate the definitions that follow.

Catcher's Mitt

Your most obvious clue that a particular mitt is for catchers only is the fact that it doesn't have separate slots for your fingers.

This type of mitt is also characterized by heavy padding because they're meant to protect the catcher's hand from the greater impact of a speeding ball.

Because of the way they're built, these mitts are generally sturdier and more durable than other types of mitt.

They're built specifically to survive all the action as well as to keep the catcher's hand from suffering trauma due to hard ball landings. Another determining feature of a catcher's mitt is a closed webbing and small pocket.

First Base

Mitts for first base are similar to a catcher's mitt because they also lack separate slots for your fingers. The difference is that they're not as heavily padded. They're pocket is also wider than a catcher's mitt, but shallower as well. This type of mitt has open webbing so as to trap the ball more easily.

Pitcher's Gloves

Just like a catcher's mitt, a pitcher's glove has closed webbing, which allows the pitcher to keep the ball hidden as he tunes up for the next pitch. This type of mitt, however, has a slot for each of your fingers.

Infielder's Gloves

The softball gloves designed for infielders are generally smaller than the average softball glove. It also features a shallower pocket, which makes it easier for the infielder to take out the ball and throw it.

This type of mitt is made with either closed or open webbing, since there are infielders who prefer closed webbing whereas others work better with open webbing.

You may want to try throwing and catching a few balls with each style to see which one you feel more comfortable using. Most third basemen prefer the mitt with closed webbing because it offers better support for hard hits.

Outfielder's Gloves

Softball mitts designed for the use of outfielders are typically the biggest and longest of all softball mitts.

The reason for their size is that outfielders are the ones responsible for catching fly balls and a bigger glove will certainly help them do just that.

Now that you have an idea regarding the different types of softball mitt and which ones are designed for which particular positions, it should be much easier for you to shop for a softball mitt of your own.

Be sure to try the mitt on at the store to ensure that it fits you just right and that you can play comfortably with it.

Being comfortable with your softball equipment and accessories goes a long way towards ensuring a good performance in the game.

Choosing Your Cleats

When you start playing softball, you'll have to buy a pair of cleats specifically designed for the sport and for the position you play.

There are basically two different forms of softball cleats: moulded or detachable.

The form of cleat you choose to wear on the field also depends on the field itself.

Some softball games are played on grass while some are played on turf. If you'll be playing on both types of field, then it's definitely a good idea to buy a pair of multipurpose cleats. As the name implies, detachable cleats are characterized by studs that you can remove or attach depending on the conditions on the field.

Wearing cleats well-suited to field conditions helps improve your performance during a game.

The type of shoes for softball cleats could be low-cut, mid-cut, or high-top.

- Low-cut cleats are best known for being lightweight and for allowing a great deal of movement on the field. They're particularly useful for times when you have to make a sudden cut.

- Mid-cut cleats are known for providing flexibility of movement. They're ideal for receivers, running back, defensive backs, and quarterbacks.

- High tops are typically chosen by players who need to make a lot of lateral movement in the course of a game. That's because continuous movement can place a great deal of pressure on your ankles and high-top cleats help ease this pressure, since they extend right up your ankles.

Softball cleats are usually made of either leather or synthetic material. Leather cleats generally offer your feet more breathing room and keep them comfortable throughout the game.

On the other hand, synthetic cleats typically cause sweating, but are generally less expensive.

Your choice of material for your cleats will therefore depend on your budget. If you can afford leather cleats, then that would definitely be the better option.

Softball cleats are also available in a wide variety of colours and though the different colours don't really do anything for your performance, they certainly make your shoes look more attractive and may even make you feel good about yourself.

Confidence is an important factor in any sport and an attractive pair of shoes can certainly add to your confidence on the field.

The good news for you is that there are various cleats available for softball players of all ages. There are also a number of good brands you can choose from.

Just like the variety of colours, the brand your softball cleats carry won't have anything to do with your performance on the field, but it certainly does a lot for your confidence and sense of well-being when you're wearing softball gear with brands you trust.

You may want to seek the advice of more experienced players or your team's coach as regards the best brands that offer quality and durability.

And though you may be able to find softball cleats for sale in online stores, it's best to shop at a physical retail store where you can actually try them on and walk around in them to ensure a perfect fit.

Four Areas to Consider

Softball is one game that requires an excellent performance from your entire body. You have to remember that every time you swing that bat or throw that ball, you aren't just using your hands and arms.

Both actions require proper coordination of your entire body in order to achieve efficiency in movement and an excellent overall performance.

Do you seriously want to become an excellent softball player?

If so, then you'll have to carefully consider the following areas:

1. **Balance**

Athletes require great balance regardless of their chosen sport, but most especially if you've chosen a game like softball. You can't expect to be very successful in your plays if you don't have a sense of balance.

Stability boards are excellent tools for developing the sense of balance that you need. It's also a good idea to engage in drills that put you in an unsteady state so you can improve the manner in which you react to the situation.

2. Flexibility

It's easy to understand why the movements associated with softball would require flexibility. You need to have a wide range of motion, which provides greater athleticism and reduces the risk for injury, particularly in your chest, hips, hamstrings, and calves.

Whatever physical fitness program you engage in, you should never forget to do some stretching exercises as part of both you warm-up and cool down routines.

3. Coordination

Whatever situation you find yourself in during a softball game, you should have the ability to react immediately without having to second guess your movements. You need to be able to hit and field a fast-paced ball.

You should also have the ability to throw the ball accurately towards the right targets. And you can only accomplish all these with excellent hand-eye and hand-to-hand coordination. Although coordination is largely a natural ability, it can also be developed using various exercises.

4. Agility and Speed

Softball naturally requires you to be quick-footed if you ever hope to build a successful career in the sport. You also need to develop the ability to quickly change direction without much break in your speed.

Additionally, you need the ability to accelerate laterally to compensate for any lapses. This is one type of sport where the tiniest improvement in your game can make a world of difference.

Softball training should therefore include footwork drills, stamina-building sessions, running strategies, and drills to increase speed and improve your ability to react instantly.

You need to remember as well as that every movement in softball requires power. Throwing, running, and hitting are all explosive movements requiring strength and a good deal of speed. This is why you need to develop your strength, balance, agility, flexibility, and coordination.

Not only do these attributes allow you to perform better in a softball game, but they also help you avoid serious injuries.

Bear in mind that when you go through your fitness routines for softball, you need to work on strengthening your torso, shoulders, and knees. You should also strive to develop proper posture while you're at it.

Hitting Better

As a beginner in the sport of softball, your reflexes may not really be in top shape yet.

The first time you get up to bat, your muscles could still be too sore from working out at intensities you aren't used to.

Of course, you can't expect to have the same skill level as the more experienced players on the team.

But, that doesn't mean you can't do anything to improve your hitting skills and become at par with them! If you've played baseball before, then it could be easier for you to learn the ropes in softball.

And the good thing is that there are a lot of weekend games being played just about anywhere, so it's quite easy to get a lot of practice in an actual game.

Although softball has many similarities to baseball, it has a number of differences as well.

For one thing, the hitting style required may be different, which is why your experience in baseball doesn't necessarily make you a good softball player.

You may need to modify your swing in order to develop excellent hitting skills in softball.

Here are some valuable tips that can assist you in developing a better softball swing:

1. Bear in mind that softball bats have a different shape, length, and weight as compared to baseball bats.

    It's critical to choose the right bat, of course and the general rule in softball is for you to go with the largest bat that allows you to swing comfortably.

    For example, if you're used to swinging with a 34" bat, but you can still swing comfortably with a 35" bat, then it's a good idea to switch to the 35".

2. Most softball players position their hands at the bottom part of the bat against the knob so as to hit with more power. If you feel more comfortable by gripping the area higher up the bat, then go for it.

    This is one of the things softball has in common with baseball.

The speed of your swing is more important than the bat's weight where hitting power is concerned.

3. Ideally, your softball swing should come from a level cut to a slightly higher cut. This provides a lift to the ball, which is actually what gives it the power that you're looking for.

   Remember that there's a fine line dividing a home run and a high pop fly towards infield, so you'll really have to practice this swing. If you want to accomplish ground balls and line drives, then you need to execute a level swing. This is best done if you're a less muscular hitter.

4. Keep your eyes on the ball and your head level as you swing. If you have baseball experience, then you're likely to have heard this advice before. You need to remember, though, that the arc and flight of a softball pitch is completely different from that of baseball.

It can be too easy for you to pull your head and take your eyes off the ball as you swing. This can result in hitting the ball right back to the pitcher, something you definitely don't want to happen.

Above all, be patient. Softball pitches are naturally slower than baseball pitches. You need to overcome the temptation of swinging too soon.

You should also be patient in applying the above tips as you slowly improve your hitting skills.

Pitching Tips

If you hope to join a softball team as a pitcher, then one of the first things you need to bear in mind is that a softball pitch requires a single fluid motion.

And while it can be difficult to coach softball pitching according to the fundamental skills, you need to gain an understanding of the mechanics that can help you develop your pitching skills.

Breaking the single pitching motion down into to the fundamentals should help improve your delivery.

Here are some tips on how to establish a strong foundation for softball pitching:

1. Grip

The manner of gripping the ball in a softball pitch will depend largely on the type of pitch you're going to throw. Take note that the manner in which you hold the ball will dictate its rotation and the seams' interaction with the wind. This interaction will then determine the speed of the ball.

If, for example, you want to deliver a four-seam fastball, you'll have to grip the ball such that its laces form a "C" and then place your fingers across that "C". Whatever type of delivery you're going to throw, remember that the ball should be held in your fingers rather than against your palm.

2. Stance

The stance is the position you assume before you start your wind-up. Although each pitcher can have a different stance, there's a basic stance you should be comfortable with and consistently execute. You should start by keeping the ball in your glove and standing upright at the pitcher's plate.

You should place your lead foot on the rubber with your toes extending over the front edge. The toes of your rear foot should then touch the back edge of the rubber. Make sure your front leg is straight and your back leg slightly bent.

Remember to keep your weight on the balls of your feet. As the catcher gives you the signal for play, you should shift your weight forward, visualize your pitch, and begin the wind-up.

3. The Windmill

The windmill method is currently the most commonly used type of delivery in softball. This is an underhand pitch where the pitcher begins with his throwing arm in front of his body. He then winds back, makes a circular motion with his arm, releases the ball at hip level, and then executes a follow through.

Take note, though, that this delivery involves more than just arm motion. It also requires the pitcher to take a long stride and generate power from his legs and torso. The speed with which the delivery is executed and the shifting of the pitcher's weight play a crucial role in effectively delivery.

4. Completing the Motion

You can't just go through the pitching motion without the follow through. This is what completes the entire movement and ensures proper execution of the delivery.

As soon as you get comfortable with your grip and stance, you'll have to move on to practicing the pitching motion itself.

It's understandable for you to feel a bit overwhelmed at first, but as long as you keep working on the basics and practicing consistently, you should soon be ready to move on to learning more advanced skills.

Strengthening Your Outfield Throw

Although the ball used in softball is much larger and the bases are positioned much closer together, the sport still requires arm strength just as much as baseball does.

In fact, arm strength is even more important for quick play, considering that everything is on a smaller scale in the softball field.

Here are a few exercises that can help you build the necessary muscle mass for increased strength in your throwing muscles.

Arm Circles

This exercise is done by standing with your feet a shoulder width apart. You then have to raise your arms sideways to shoulder height and then start rotating forwards for 15 seconds, after which you should reverse the rotation for another 15 seconds.

The last step is to drop your arms and then shake them out. It's advisable to do ten repetitions of this exercise each day. You'd also do well to increase the duration of the rotations by five seconds each day until you reach your maximum endurance.

This should help you develop balance, flexibility, stamina, and endurance.

Jobe Exercise

This exercise takes its name from the person who developed it, Frank Jobe. It was originally designed as part of the rehabilitation routine for an arm injury, but soon started to be used for regular strength training. It is performed by standing with your feet a shoulder width apart.

Grab a 1- to 3-pound weight in each of your hands, which should be positioned at your side.

Raise your arms slowly sideways to shoulder level and then lower them back down slowly to your side.

Do three sets of this exercise with ten repetitions each. As your strength increases, you may increase the number of repetitions as well or the amount of the weight.

Take note, though, that you shouldn't go beyond five pounds so as not to suffer from muscle stress.

Long Toss Exercise

As its name indicates, this exercise involves throwing the ball farther and farther as you gain more and more strength. It's advisable to start the exercise by throwing the ball 50' away and then increasing the distance by 10' until you're able to throw at a distance of 100' or 100'.

Take note that it's not just the distance that makes this exercise effective.

The frequency of your throws and the total number of throws you make also influences the level of success you achieve with it.

It's best throw for greater distances with less number of throws and more sessions.

Just like any other exercise, you should always do some stretching before and after performing the above exercises, particularly the long toss. Stretching should be a permanent part of your warm-up and cool down routines in order to reduce your risk for injury.

Remember as well that the above exercises in no way constitute a complete strength conditioning program for softball, since they only work your arms.

Your torso and your legs also play a crucial role in the sport and should therefore be developed along with your arms.

Running the Bases

Learning how to run the bases properly is extremely important in the sport of softball, especially since lead offs aren't allowed in this sport.

Take note that in a sport such as softball, smart runners can be just as effective as fast runners, and maybe even more so.

The strategies used in running from the home plate to first base are similar to those used in baseball.

That is, you should run as hard as you can through the base and veer towards the right as soon as you hit the bag. You should also remember not to slow down as you approach first base.

The same strategy is also used to gain an extra base hit, wherein you swing out in the direction of the dugout to hit the inside of first base and then run in a straight line towards second base.

And when you're already on first base, you're next goal is also similar to that of baseball, which is to advance to the next bases.

This time, however, the strategies you need to use in order to achieve your goal should be different, since leadoffs aren't allowed.

There are generally two ways in which you can smartly move on to second base.

The most important thing for you to bear in mind is that you can't leave the base when the ball hasn't left the hands of the pitcher yet.

Timing is therefore extremely critical. The first strategy you may want to try is to position your left foot on the back part of the base.

Your right arm should then lead towards second base and your body should be cocked towards the pitcher. As the ball is released, you should push off with your left leg and move forward three steps.

Make sure you're always facing the ball so you can immediately move to second base or get back to first as necessary.

The second strategy involves placing your right leg against the front part of the base and then using your left arm as the lead.

Just like the first strategy, you may take three steps forward as the ball leaves the pitcher's hands.

The decision as to which method you use depends largely on your personal preference. You may use the same strategies for leading off from second to third base.

What's important is for you to remember the "shortest distance" rule in situations where you need to get to third base really quickly. This means you need to lead off in a straight line towards third base, since a straight path gives you the shortest distance between second and third base.

If your ultimate goal is to score, then you'd do well to take your usual lead off and then veering off a little towards left field so you can "cut" third base by simply hitting the inside corner with your foot before proceeding in a direct line to home plate.

If you need to lead off from third base to home plate, make sure that your shoulders are square to the infield so you can quickly return to the base whenever necessary.

With enough practice, you should be able to execute these strategies effectively and properly run the bases in softball.

Improving Vision

In the sport of softball, vision involves more than just your eyesight. It also involves your ability to perceive such factors as location, motion, and rotation either at the plate or on the field.

Even if you currently have 20/20 eyesight, your vision may still have room for improvement.

The good news is that there are a number of exercises that can help you improve your vision and you can perform these exercises as part of your softball practice drills.

Accurate vision is very important in every aspect of a softball game. As a softball player, you need to keep making quick decisions and your vision will definitely affect your ability to make the right decisions on the field.

When you get up to bat, you'll have to decide if you should swing or not depending on the direction, speed, and rotation of the ball. And if you do decide to swing, you'll have to decide how.

When you run the bases, you'll have to decide whether to stay on base or run and you'll have to determine when you can possibly steal a base.

When fielding fly balls or grounders, you need to where to meet and throw the ball. In all of these decisions, it certainly helps to have good vision, which you can successfully develop using these drills:

1. Colour/Number Drill

Ask a friend to write down the numbers 0 through 9 on practice balls using a permanent marker. You may use differently-coloured markers if you want. As you practice hitting, you'll have to identify each ball before taking a swing.

You can progress through the drill by first identifying just the colour of the ball and then moving on to identifying the number.

As you become more adept, you may progress to identifying both colour and number. And if you want to challenge yourself even more, then you could increase the speed of the pitch.

2. Coloured Ball Drill

Mark your practice balls using different colours. You should then swing according to the designated action for each of the colours.

For example, for balls marked black, you should hit away; for balls marked red, you shouldn't swing; and for balls marked blue, you should bunt.

The actions you assign for each colour depends on your personal preference, of course.

The good thing about trying to improve your vision is that you can also work on it even when you're at home. You could perform simple exercises such as training your eyes to switch their focus from one object to another.

For example, you could stare at your computer screen and then switch your gaze to a painting hanging from the wall across the room.

In time, your vision accuracy and focus time should improve significantly. You could even work on your vision while you're driving.

Focus on your dashboard for a few seconds and then quickly switch your gaze to the plate number of the car in front of you. There are just so many things you can do to improve your vision for softball.

Sliding Basics

Sliding is one of the crucial moves in softball that beginners are a bit reluctant to try. Such hesitation often stems from the fear of getting injured or hurt in any way.

In most cases, you'll never be able to overcome this fear unless you actually try to execute a slide.

Fortunately, there are ways for you to learn how to slide easily enough and without getting hurt.

Following are some guidelines on how to execute the softball slide such that you become more comfortable with it and can start using it whenever you need to.

The Stance

Just like in any other skill, the stance is the first thing you need to learn in sliding.

Start learning how to slide by sitting down on the ground with your legs extended in front of you.

Fold one knee and then the other to determine which position you're more comfortable with.

You should then extend one of your legs with your foot pointing towards the base and bend the other at the knee with your foot pointing behind you.

You should then raise both of your hands in the air. While it may be tempting to do so, you should refrain from putting your hands down, as that will increase your risk for injury.

Sliding

Your first attempts at softball sliding can be made much easier by doing them on a wet field. You could douse the field with a garden hose or sprinkler, or practice right after it has rained. A wet surface definitely makes it a lot easier for you to slide than a hard and dry surface does.

This is why sliding on wet grass during your first few attempts is often advised. If you're feeling a bit adventurous, you could use a slip and slide.

Place a water hose on top of a piece of plastic to wet it down and then practice your slide on it during a hot day.

Remember that it's best to wear grungy clothes for sliding practice.

Scrambled Eggs Drill

If you've learned the basic softball sliding position, but you're still having trouble remembering to keep your hands in the air as you do so, then this is the perfect drill for you. It'll definitely help you maintain the right stance for sliding.

As the name implies, this drill is performed using eggs. Specifically, you need about two dozen raw eggs for the drill. What you basically have to do is keep sliding into bases while holding an egg in each of your hands.

The goal is for you to successfully slide into the bases without breaking any of the eggs. That should force you to hold your hands high up in the air!

To add to the challenge of the drill, you could try sliding really low or sliding into a base and then getting up immediately to sprint to the next base.

You have to keep the eggs safe while doing all these, of course. Every time you break an egg, grab another one and start over.

Improving Technique

The best practice drills for softball players are those that allow you to learn new techniques while also giving you the opportunity to review your progress and training results over time.

When you use these drills effectively, they should provide you with enough challenge such that your strength increases and you're able to perform better whatever position you play for your team.

Here are some softball training drills that help you strengthen your base running, infield, and outfield techniques:

Two-Line Challenge

This softball drill helps you improve your infield catching skills and also includes diving practice in most cases. The team forms two lines, with one line at shortstop position and the other at second base.

Your coach will then stand in the middle and roll the ball in either direction. The first player in the chosen line then fields the ball, which could require diving for it. He will then toss the ball back to the coach and move to the back of the line.

In-Betweens

This drill helps outfielders learn the value of communication as they work on successfully catching fly balls. Your team is divided into two groups, with each group forming a line in the outfield.

You need to spread out to cover around 60 feet. Your coach will then stand in front and throw a ball into the air such that it travels like a fly ball. The two players at the head of each line are tasked to call for the ball and catch it. They will then move to the back of the line so the next two players can perform the drill.

Base Cycles

This particular drill helps increase your speed and improve your base running technique. Your team needs to form a single line at home plate. The fastest player should stand at the head of the line and the slowest at the end.

Each player then has to run from home plate through first base, making sure there's a safe distance between players.

As soon as all players have reached first base, the team has to line up again and then run to second base. The process is repeated until all players get to run from third base back to home plate.

Finally, you could perform a drill that's similar to base cycles, but this time each player runs from home plate straight through second base. After lining up once again at second base, the players then run to third base and straight back to home plate.

What's important in performing these last two drills is for each of the players on your team to concentrate on executing the proper base running technique. You should also focus on following the specific instructions of your base coaches.

As long as you go through these drills consistently and with dedication, you should be able to see your softball skills improve much faster than you first thought.

Just like anything else in the world, practice is the key to perfecting your softball moves.

Fitness Training

Experts now agree that weight training can definitely help softball players improve their overall game.

And specific weight training programs have even been developed for the sport. The training programs designed for softball players primarily focus on core stability.

They serve to provide you with the power conditioning you need for excellent performance in the game.

These programs typically take about four to six weeks to complete and it's important for them to be done along with a complete body workout.

The sad thing is that many softball players limit their muscle strengthening workout by working only on specific muscle groups at a time.

Bear in mind that it's essential for all of your major muscle groups to be included in your strengthening routines.

You should never take your upper body, abdominal muscles, lower back, hip abductors, hip adductors, and hip flexors for granted.

The value of exercising and strengthening all of these muscle groups lies in the fact that it helps you avoid injury.

Here are some of the exercises you need to include in your softball training program:

1. Stork Stance

This exercise works on your balance and core stability. You perform it by standing on your left leg with your knee bent a little. As soon as you achieve this position, you need to draw your belly button towards your spine.

Extend your right leg behind you as you slowly bend at the waist. Keep your right leg straight as much as you can and maintain this position as you lift your arms such that they're parallel to the floor. Repeat the exercise on the other leg.

2. Horse Stance

In performing this exercise, you need to drop to your hands and knees, keeping your spine in a neutral position. Tuck your chin and draw your abdomen in.

Next, raise one arm and the opposite leg slowly. Make sure your arm is raised in a thumbs-up gesture.

Keep the raised arm and leg straight as you lift your entire body to a predetermined height and then hold the position for five to ten seconds.

Slowly bring your body as well as your arm and leg back to the ground and then repeat with the other arm and leg. As your strength increases, you may hold the position longer or perhaps add weights.

3. Cobra Stance

This exercise is designed to work your upper and lower back as well as your core and gluteus muscles. It is performed by lying face-down on the floor with your core and gluteus muscles tense.

Retract your shoulder blades slowly and then squeeze your gluteus muscles. Be sure to hold your arms by your side with your thumbs facing the ceiling.

Tuck your chin towards your chest while keeping your spine and neck properly aligned.

Never allow your head to extend backwards. You should feel a bit of discomfort in your lower back as you concentrate on the act of squeezing your gluteus muscles.

As long as you perform these three exercises regularly, you should soon see some amazing results in your softball skills and your overall game.

And if you keep up your training program, then you'll surely leave all the competition behind.

Made in the USA
Lexington, KY
10 January 2014